# IT'S ORFF SHOWTIME!

## (Orff) Performance Pieces for Different Ages

## Konnie Saliba

## Preface

Music teachers are always being asked to create performances. These can be for special times of the year, or just because nothing shows off a school better than children singing, playing and dancing. ***It's Orff Showtime!*** is a collection of performance pieces. There are four selections for lower elementary that incorporate instruments for special words in a song, games, puppets and improvisation activities.

Sometimes it is a wise idea to show parents and others what students did to prepare for the performance. For younger students, "Wake Up" is an illustration of how, beginning with words, adding special words on body percussion, transferring these words to barred and non-pitched percussion and finally, using no words at all creates a musical sound color orchestration. For older students, "Jungle Rondo" is a more sophisticated rhythmic experience. It would be good on a program to show the A, B and C sections using speech, body percussion, and finally the drums and other instruments that create this exciting rhythm orchestration.

Songs and speech pieces taught in the classroom are frequently not very long. This book features suggestions for performing a song or speech piece that will ensure that the piece lasts more than just a minute!

***It's Orff Showtime!*** is divided into five sections:

The **Lower Elementary** section contains three songs and a speech piece.

There are three speech pieces for **Middle Grades**.

Activities in the sections **Different Parts of the World** and **Songs and Dances from the U.S.A.** all have orchestrations and dances.

In the **Showstoppers** section, the "Safari Song" and "The Little Train of Dillsboro" can easily be extended to five minutes or more in length.

It was fun creating this book. I hope you enjoy it!

# TABLE OF CONTENTS

# Lower Elementary

## A Mouse in Our House

Konnie Saliba

+ any two notes in F pentatonic (remove B's and E's)

*Singing, special words, puppets, and improvisation on non-pitched percussion.*

### Performance Suggestions

® Create a box taller than the students that three students can stand behind.

® Using something similar to a wooden paint stirrer, create the following hand-held puppets: a mouse, a house, and a sleeping person.

® Use these non-pitched percussion instruments:

| | |
|---|---|
| Mouse = Finger Cymbals | House = Small Woods |
| Sleeping = Small Metals | Creeping = Cabasa |

### Form

® Sing the song once with accompaniment.

® Repeat, during which the mouse puppet appears above the box each time the special word is sung.

® Without accompaniment, finger cymbals improvise for the length of the song.

® Repeat again, and this time the mouse and house puppets will appear in appropriate places.

® Follow this with improvisation on finger cymbals and small woods.

® Repeat song again with the mouse, house, and sleeping person puppets appearing in appropriate places.

® Follow this with improvisation on finger cymbals, small woods and small metals.

® Repeat song again with the mouse, house, sleeping person and creeping puppets appearing in appropriate places (mouse puppet can move).

® Follow with improvisation on all non-pitched percussion instruments.

® Sing song one last time, during which all the puppets dance above the box for entire song.

## A Cricket Named Joe

Konnie Saliba

Verse 2: I had another cricket, his name was Jake,
He had a problem, because he liked to shake...
Verse 3: I had another cricket, his name was Mort,
He had a problem, because he was so short...
Verse 4: I had another cricket, his name was Chip,
He had a problem, because he liked to skip...
Extension: Have students create additional names and verses.

## Performance Suggestions

This song features singing, accompaniment, playing recorder and a partner game.
- ® Divide students into groups to play barred instruments and soprano recorders, and the rest into partners for the game.
- ® Partner Game: Partners are free in space, facing one another
  (One motion = quarter note ♩)

| Measure 1: | Pat knees, clap own hands, clap partner's hands, rest |
|---|---|
| Measure 2: | Clap partner's hands, clap own hands, pat knees, rest |
| Measure 3: | Repeat measure 1 |
| Measure 4: | Repeat measure 2 |
| Measure 5: | Stretch arms out from sides of body, imitating a big singing gesture |
| Measure 6: | Wiggle shoulders |
| Measures 7 & 8: | In place, do a tap dance-like step |

## Form

- ® Verse 1: Singing, accompaniment and game:
- ® Repeat melody, this time on soprano recorder, without singing and conga part; partners separate and create slow movements to a new partner.
- ® Verse 2: Singing, accompaniment and game:
- ® Repeat melody, again on soprano recorder, minus singing and conga; partners separate and create movements that allow the body to shake.
- ® Verse 3: Follow by movement low to the ground.
- ® Verse 4: Follow by skipping movement, creating one circle that moves counterclockwise.
- ® Coda: Movers move into the circle in four slow, half note steps, raising hands towards the center, then move out in four slow, half note steps, lowering arms. Add a final "HEY!" on beat four.

# Piggie Pig

Konnie Saliba

*Singing, Elimination of Words, Substituting Gestures, Group Improvisation*

## Performance Suggestions

® Substitute Gestures:

After the song is learned, add the following gestures:

| Words | Gestures |
| --- | --- |
| I've got a | *Point to self* |
| Fav'rite pet | *Stroke left arm with left hand* |
| Her name is | *Write a name in the air* |
| Piggie Pig | *Push nose* |
| She smiles, she plays | *Smile and create a playful gesture* |
| She giggles | *Silent laugh* |
| She eats corn | *Imitate eating corn on the cob* |
| So she will grow big | *Puff up body to look fat* |

® Have students place all barred instruments in F pentatonic (B's and E's removed).

® Have some students play the accompaniment and provide improvisations while others do the gestures.

## Form

® Sing the song once with accompaniment, without gestures.
® Follow this with group improvisation on glockenspiels (without accompaniment).
® Substitute the first measure with a gesture, without singing, with accompaniment.
® Follow this with group improvisation on xylophones (without accompaniment).
® Substitute the first two measures with gestures, without singing, with accompaniment.
® Follow this with group improvisation on metallophones (without accompaniment).
® Repeat the elimination of words substituted by gestures, followed by group improvisation; there will be nine improvisations in all.
® The last time the song is sung, all gestures are included.

# Wake Up

Konnie Saliba

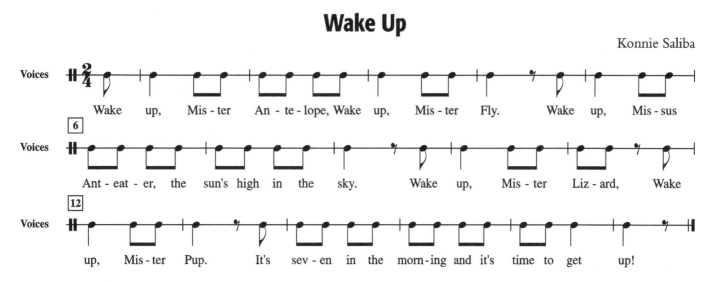

*Words Transferred to Body Percussion and Instruments, with Creative Introduction*

## Teaching Suggestions

® Display words on a visual.
® Ask students to put instruments in C Pentatonic (F's and B's removed).
® Indicate the following special words with such things as circles, squares, etc.

| | | |
|---|---|---|
| Wake up | Missus Anteater | Mister Pup |
| Mister Antelope | Sun's | Seven in the Morning |
| Mister Fly | Mister Lizard | Get Up |

® Ask for volunteers to speak each phrase in a unique way (Examples: high voice, whisper, etc.).
® Transfer each special word—from the first "Wake Up" to "Seven in the Morning"—to a different level of body percussion.
® For the words "Seven in the Morning," ask students to play any two notes from the lowest to the highest part of the barred instrument.
® For the words "Get Up," ask students to play from low C to F.
® Transfer each special word to a non-pitched percussion instrument.

## Performance Suggestions

® For introduction, ask students to provide soft tremolos on barred instruments and improvise sounds they might hear early in the morning. This could include such things as crickets, bird sounds, water and wind.
® For performance, do a creative introduction of improvised sounds, followed by poetic speech using group voices or individuals, body percussion and words, and finally no words, only instruments.

## Middle Grades and Up

## Three Little Monkeys

Text: Anonymous
Arr. Konnie Saliba

Verse 2: Two little monkeys…
Verse 3: One little monkey…
After the word "SNAP!" insert the words "MISSED ME!"

### Performance Suggestions

® Dance:
Form lines of partners, facing each other

| (One movement and body percussion = quarter note ♩) | |
|---|---|
| Measures 1 & 2: | Side-Close, Side-Close, Side-Close, Side-Touch (to the right) |
| Measures 3 & 4: | Side-Close, Side-Close, Side-Close, Side-Touch (to the left) |
| Measure 5: | Pat, Clap own hands, Clap partner's hands, Clap own hands |
| Measure 6: | Pat, Clap own hands, Clap partner's hands, Rest |
| Measure 7: | Exchange places with partner, passing right shoulders in four steps |
| Measure 8: | Clap, Snap, Clap, Snap |

® Transfer the rhythm of the words in Measures 1-5 to hand drums.
® Transfer Measure 6 to triangle.
® Transfer the word "SNAP!" to "WHIP!"
® Perform speaking Verse 1 with movement and accompaniment.
® Perform with non-pitched percussion, movement and accompaniment.
® Repeat the above with the other two verses; six times in all.

# Jungle Rondo

Konnie Saliba

## Teaching Suggestion

® Create a visual and teach the rhythms of each rondo section with words.

## Form

® During the A Section, encourage students playing the hand drum part to play accents on the lower part of the drum.

® To create a crescendo and provide a more exciting performance, begin with small hand drums, and increase the numbers and sizes of drums every two measures.

® During the B Section, suggest that students use a scraping sound on guiro for the words "big, big, tall, tall," and a tapping sound for "spotted giraffe."

® For the C Section:

1) Begin with the "orangutan ostinato" only.

2) After two patterns, the "tiger ostinato" enters.

3) After two more patterns, the "elephant ostinato" enters.

4) After two more patterns, the clapping rhythm enters.

® In the piece, the "orangutan ostinato" is played eight times, the "tiger ostinato" six times, the "elephant ostinato" four times, and the clapping rhythm two times.

## Performance Suggestions

® To extend the work, perform a symmetrical rondo (ABACABA), and follow this with one more repeat that combines the A, B, and C Sections, ending the piece on beat three of the A Section.

# You Can Do It Too!

Konnie Saliba

*Words can be used as concrete ways to present new material. Below are ways these three ostinatos might be demonstrated in class.*

## Performance Suggestions

| Speech |
|---|
| Ask students to speak each pattern twice.  Insist upon interesting vocal inflection. |
| Ostinato 1 = Crescendo |
| Ostinato 2 = Staccato |
| Ostinato 3 = Use high voices for Line 1, middle voices for Line 2 and low voices for Line 3. |
| Divide the students into three groups; begin with Ostinato 1, layer Ostinato 2 on top and then add Ostinato 3. |

| Body Percussion |
|---|
| Transfer each pattern to body percussion: |
| Ostinato 1 = Clapping with a crescendo |
| Ostinato 2 = Patting knees |
| Ostinato 3 = Snap Line 1, clap Line 2 and stamp Line 3. |
| Repeat: Perform the patterns singly and then in a layered ensemble. |

| Non-Pitched Percussion Instruments |
|---|
| Transfer each pattern to non-pitched percussion instruments: |
| Ostinato 1 = Small woods |
| Ostinato 2 = Bongos and congas |
| Ostinato 3 = Triangle on Line 1, hand drums on Line 2 and bass drum on Line 3 |

**Notes**

# Songs and Dances from Different Parts of the World

## Mama Paquita

Brazilian Carnival Song
Arr. Konnie Saliba

joy Ma-ma Ma - ma        Let's go to    car - ni-val and    dance the night a - way.
joy Ma-ma-Ma - ma        Let's go to    car - ni-val and    dance the night a - way.

## Movement

® Partners join and cross hands, moving counterclockwise in the circle.

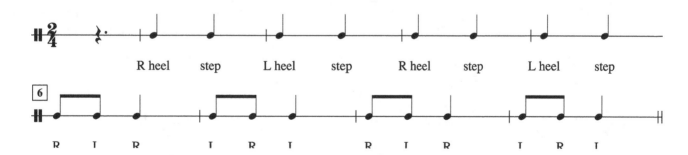

R heel        step        L heel        step        R heel        step        L heel        step

R  I  R        I  R  I        R  I  R        I  R  I

## Performance Suggestions

® Ask the students to create an improvised introduction for the carnival.  This could include tremolos on barred instruments (in C pentatonic remove F's and B's), street cries, improvised recorder music, couples dancing and talking, etc.

® On a cue, the sound diminishes and sixteen measures of accompaniment prepare the dancers to get into circle formation.

® To extend the performance, consider singing, playing and moving for a verse as well as repeating without singing.

## Stone Pounding

Jamaican Folk Song
Arr. Konnie Saliba

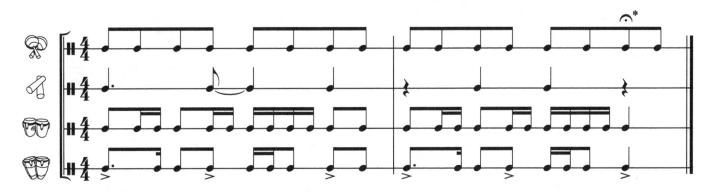

## Performance Suggestions

| Dance: Line Formation |
| --- |
| Teach students this samba-like dance: |
| On beat one, the right foot is always somewhat in front of the left foot; repeat with the left foot in front (or see below) |
| Tell the students to pretend they are gently stepping into a hole on the first eighth note, then stepping back to the other foot on the second eighth note. |
| Girls shake their skirts while boys put their hands behind their backs. |

® Begin with eight measures of non-pitched percussion.

® Sing and dance with accompaniment.

## Form

® To extend the performance, repeat the melody, without singing, playing it on alto and soprano xylophones.

® Add sections in which non-pitched percussion players improvise for sixteen measures. During the improvisation, dancers can move out of line formation and dance freely in space, returning to lines to repeat the A Section.

*Note: On beat one, the right foot is somewhat in front of the left foot. Use the above rhythm ( ♫ ♩).*
*Repeat the rhythm and steps, starting with the left foot slightly in front of the right.*

## Thank You for the Chris'mus

Jamaican Folk Song
Arr. Konnie Saliba

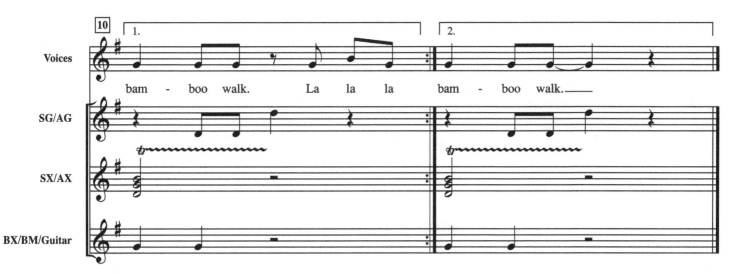

(tremolo all three notes for SX/AX part)

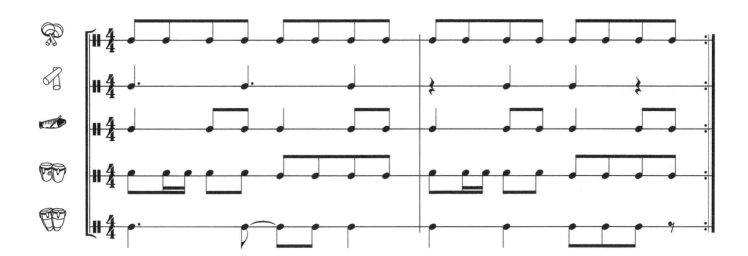

## Performance Suggestions

| Dance | |
|---|---|
| Use the samba-like step described with the song "Stone Pounding." The dance can be varied by creating small groups moving in serpentine lines freely in space. | |
| In addition to the step, add the following arm movements: | |
| **Measures 1 & 2:** | Hold right arm straight up on the right side of the body with elbow slightly bent. Put fingers of the left hand under the right elbow. |
| **Measures 3 & 4:** | Do as in Measures 1 & 2, but with the left arm up and motions reversed. |
| **Variation:** | Roll hands around one another in front of body, chest level, two measures forward roll, two measures backward. |

® Because the song is short, suggest to students that they create additional verses regarding things for which they are thankful.

® For the soprano xylophone/alto xylophone tremolos, divide the chords so that players are playing two of the three notes.

## Form

® To extend the performance, begin with eight measures of the accompaniment, or with non-pitched percussion only.

® Sing the song with accompaniment, without dancers.

® Repeat, playing melody on recorders or alto and soprano xylophones; at this time, dancers enter from side of stage.

® Repeat song with accompaniment and dance.

® Repeat song with accompaniment, dance and soprano recorders or xylophones.

# Months of the Year

French Folk Song
Arr. Konnie Saliba

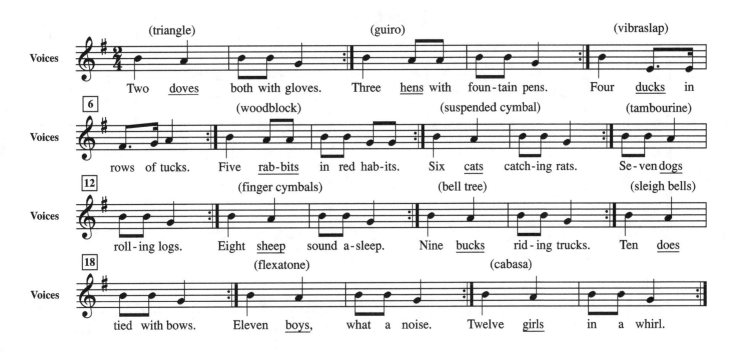

## Performance Suggestions

- ® Each underlined character has a designated non-pitched instrument, to be played when the character is named.
- ® All additions are accompanied by tremolos on low E by alto and bass instruments.
- ® Each of the additions can be sung by a different soloist.
- ® Students could create hand puppets for each character.
- ® As another choice, the flute/soprano recorder part can be played on an alto xylophone.

## Form

- ® The form is additive in the same way as the familiar song "The Twelve Days of Christmas."
- ® After singing through the first verse, return to the A Section and repeat with extra verses, i.e. "Two doves both with gloves," "Three hens with fountain pens," etc., until all twelve characters have been added.

# Zhankoye

Yiddish Folk Song
Arr. Konnie Saliba

## Performance Suggestions

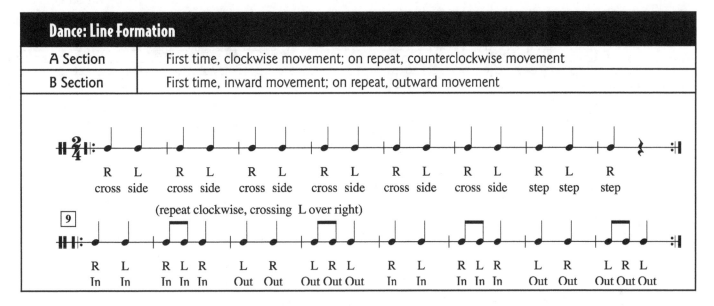

| Dance: Line Formation | |
| --- | --- |
| A Section | First time, clockwise movement; on repeat, counterclockwise movement |
| B Section | First time, inward movement; on repeat, outward movement |

® Melody can be played on soprano recorder, flute or clarinet.

® Countermelody can be played on flute, soprano recorder, clarinet or alto xylophone.

® Experiment with different melodic combinations.

## Form

| To Extend the Performance | | |
| --- | --- | --- |
| Begin without dancers. | | |
| During the A Section, play: | Melody with accompaniment | |
| | Countermelody with accompaniment | |
| | Both melody and countermelody | |
| Repeat the above sequence in the B Section. | | |
| Repeat the above two sequences and have dancers enter from a side stage or the back of the performance area. | | |

# Traditional Kalevala Melody

Finnish Folk Song
Arr. Konnie Saliba

## Dance: Circle Formation, Hands Held

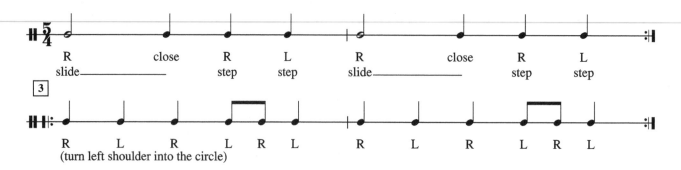

## Performance Suggestions

® Optional headdresses with waist-length ribbons hanging down the back may be worn by dancers.

® The tempo is very slow ($\quad$ = 69), and the dance should be stately.

® The melody can be played on a soprano recorder or flute; however, it could also be plucked on traditional string instruments, psaltery or lap dulcimer.

® The countermelody can be performed on alto xylophone or clarinet; the melody should sound one octave higher than the countermelody.

® A hand drum played with a hard mallet can be used.

® Experiment with different melodic combinations.

## Form

To extend the performance, use this suggested form:

- ® Perform the A Section with melody and accompaniment; with countermelody and accompaniment; with both melody and countermelody.
- ® Perform the B Section with melody and accompaniment; with countermelody and accompaniment; with both melody and countermelody.
- ® Repeat all of the above.

## Background

This five note melody can be played on a *kantele*, a small stringed instrument used for hundreds of years, and a national symbol of Finland. While the traditional *kantele* has five strings that are plucked, the modern version varies from twelve to forty-six strings.

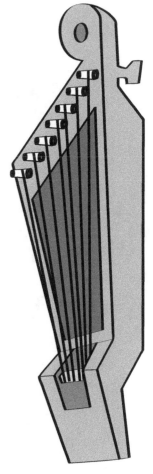

# Songs and Dances from the U.S.A.

## Goodbye Girls, I'm Going to Boston

American Folk Song
Arr. Konnie Saliba

## Performance Suggestions

| Dance | |
|---|---|
| Instruct students to move in a circle formation with hands held high, moving counterclockwise. | |
| (One step = quarter note ♩) | |
| Measures 1-4: | Step R, slide L (four times in all) |
| Measures 5-8: | Repeat measures 1-4, moving clockwise |
| Measures 9-10: | In, in, in, touch |
| Measures 11-12: | Out, out, out, touch |
| Measures 13-14: | In, in, in, touch |
| Measures 15-16: | Out, out, out, close |

## Form

- ® Sing and dance with accompaniment.
- ® Repeat with melody played on soprano recorder, dulcimers or a fiddle.
- ® Sing and dance with accompaniment.
- ® Repeat with melody played on soprano xylophones.
- ® To extend the performance, let the students create a hand/clap partner game to use as a B section.

## Oh, Mister Sun

American Folk Song
Arr. Konnie Saliba

## Creative Activity

® Ask students to survey friends or relatives who know how to do the "jitterbug." Those students who learn a step can share with others in the class. Choreograph a jitterbug-like dance combining ideas from different students.

## Performance Suggestions

® Sing and dance with the accompaniment.

® Play melody on soprano xylophones (some with hard mallets) with dancing and singing.

® Repeat the above steps several times.

# Notes

# Happiness Runs

American Folk Song
Arr. Konnie Saliba

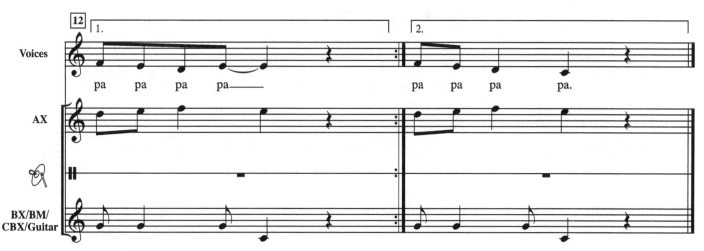

\* suggestion: perform the melody in a "jazzy" swing style

## Performance Suggestions

| Dance: Line Formation | |
|---|---|
| Measure 1: | Take two "jazzy" steps to the right. |
| Measure 2: | Take two "jazzy" steps to the left. |
| Measure 3: | Take two "jazzy" steps forward. |
| Measure 4: | Take two "jazzy" steps back. |

Repeat the above steps throughout the song, or ask students to create another movement sequence for the B Section, which starts with "pa-pa."

## Form

® Sing and move with accompaniment.

® Repeat and add alto xylophone and soprano glockenspiel/alto glockenspiel for the B Section.

® Without singing, play the A and B melodies on soprano xylophone; or play the A melody on soprano recorder and the B melody on soprano xylophone.

® Add improvised movements to the repeats that are only instrumental.

## Ain't That A-Rockin'

South Carolina Folk Song
Arr. Konnie Saliba

## Performance Suggestions

For movements, have students stand in a circle with hands held.

- During the A Section, the circle moves forward counterclockwise and backward clockwise.
- During the B Section, make hands free and move the circle in to the center and out away from the center. Students may also create their own movements for this section.

## Form

- Sing the song with accompaniment and movement.
- Play the melody on soprano recorders or flute, with accompaniment and movement.
- To extend the performance, have a few students create a sixteen bar rhythm improvisation on instruments such as congas, tambourines, and claves. Students who are moving may also create individual improvisations freely in space, returning to the circle in measure sixteen.
- Sing the song again, adding improvisations, with and without accompaniment.

## Peace Like a River

African American Spiritual
Arr. Konnie Saliba

Verse 2: I've got joy like a fountain…
Verse 3: I've got love like an ocean…

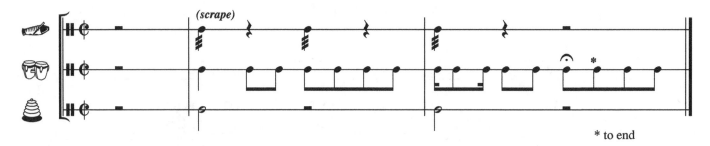

*\* to end*

## Performance Suggestions

® For movement, have students form a circle, holding hands.

| Verse 1 | |
|---|---|
| Measures 1-8: | Slowly raise hands for 4 measures, then lower hands for 4 measures. |
| Verse 2 | |
| Measures 1-8: | On the word "joy," silently clap hands and make a large circle in the air. |
| Verse 3 | |
| Measures 1-8: | Rejoin hands and sway right to left in a half note pulse. |

## Form

® To extend the form, each verse can be sung, then followed by an instrumental melody on soprano recorder, flute or oboe.

® Use guiro only in Verse 1, guiro and bongos in Verse 2, and guiro, bongos and bell tree in Verse 3.

# Wayfaring Stranger

American Folk Song
Arr. Konnie Saliba

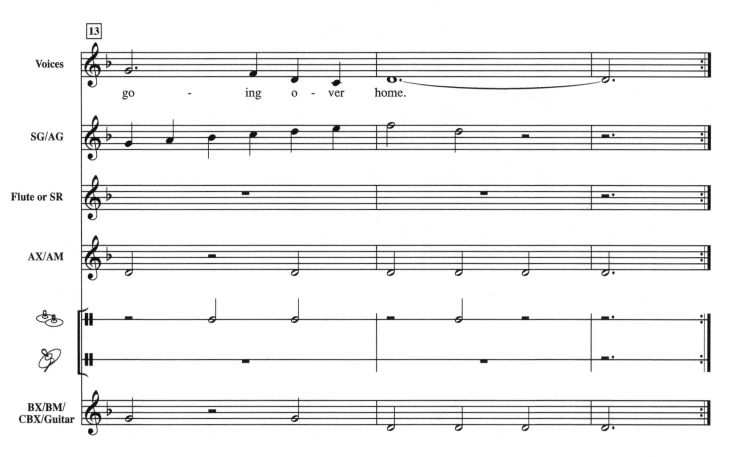

Verse 3:
I know dark clouds with gather 'round me,
I know my way is rough and steep.
But golden fields lie out before me,
Where all the saints their vigils keep.
(chorus)

## Performance Suggestions

® In Verses 2, 3, and 4, change the word "father" to "mother," "sister" or "brother."

® Some verses may be performed by soloists.

® The melody can be played on soprano recorders and/or barred instruments.

## Form

® To extend the performance, put barred instruments in D minor pentatonic (E's and B's removed), and allow for group or individual improvisation between verses.

# Our Meeting Is Over

American Folk Song
Arr. Konnie Saliba

Verse 2: Mothers
Verse 3: Sisters
Verse 4: Brothers

## Performance Suggestions

® For movements, have students form a double circle of partners, moving counterclockwise

® Have partners hold each other's hands while performing these steps:

(One step = half note ♩)

| A Section |
| --- |
| Step forward with right foot, step forward with left foot, step forward with right foot, touch left toe in the middle of the circle |
| Step back with left foot, step back with right foot, step back with left foot, touch right toe toward outside of circle |
| Repeat: Right foot, left foot, right foot, touch |
| Repeat: Left foot, right foot, left foot, then turn to face partner |
| **B Section** |
| In measure 9, on the word "land," both circles slide to the right in time, shaking hands twice with a new partner on the word "shore." Repeat the movement three more times. |
| Everyone keeps their new partner for a repeat of the A Section. |

® This song can be used to end a program or conference.

® The flute countermelody can also be played on soprano recorder.

® The soprano and alto glockenspiel parts can be played on soprano xylophones and soprano metallophones, and the flute part can be played on soprano and alto glockenspiels.

® Guitar can be added, playing G major, D minor or F major chords.

# Showstoppers

## Safari Song

American Folk Song
Arr. Konnie Saliba

* use hard mallets

sing and move and play in our Sa - far - i song!
sing and move and play in our Sa - far - i song!

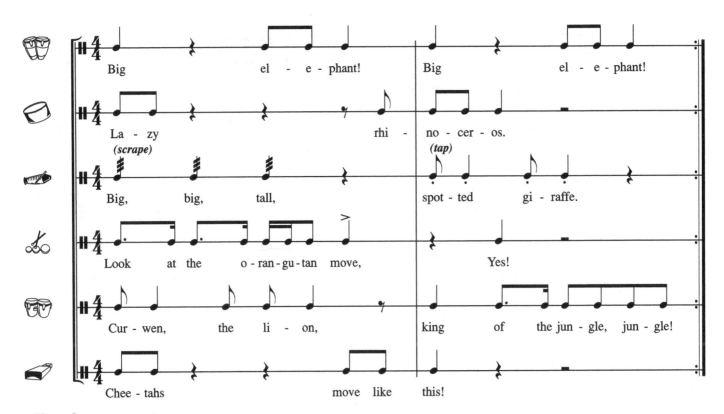

Verse 2:
We took a trip to the Memphis Zoo,
To visit the animals and see what they do.
We asked them to come along,
To sing and move and play in our Safari song!
Verse 3:
Here come the animals, one by one.
They all want to join us for some animal fun.
They all want to come along,
To sing and move and play in our Safari song!

## Performance Suggestions

® Have students who are playing animal sounds on non-pitched percussion enter the performance area from a hidden position (see "Introduction of Animals" below).

® For maximum effect, suggest that students mime the way the animal walks and behaves and maintain this throughout the performance. For example, a student's arm can be used to mimic an elephant's trunk, which can then hold a mallet to play the conga.

® Students playing animal sounds on non-pitched percussion may also make masks to wear of the animal they represent.

## Form

® Introduction: Play 8 measures of the accompaniment.
® Verse 1: Perform with singing and accompaniment.
® Interlude: Play the melody on soprano recorders, with accompaniment.
® Verse 2: Perform with singing and accompaniment.
® Repeat Interlude.

After the second interlude, all accompaniment stops and students speak in an excited voice, "HERE THEY COME!"

| Introduction of Animals |
| --- |
| **Begin with the "big elephant" and repeat these steps to introduce all the animals:** |
| 1. Have performers speak the animal's ostinato while the "elephant" moves from offstage to its respective non-pitched instrument. |
| 2. Performers drop out, and the "animal" solos on its ostinato two more times on its instrument. At the end of the solo, the next animal is announced. |
| 3. Repeat this format for the "lazy rhinoceros." After the solo, the "elephant" joins in and plays along with the "rhinoceros" for two more repetitions, before moving on to the next animal. |
| 4. Continue with this format until all the animals are onstage, and all ostinatos are being performed simultaneously. |
| 5. After the last animal has been introduced, continue repeating ostinatos and add the melody on soprano recorders and accompaniment. |

® Verse 3: Perform with singing, accompaniment, animal ostinatos and melody on soprano recorders.

® Interlude

® Repeat Verse 3.

® On beat four of the last measure, end the piece by having the group shout "YEH!"

# The Little Train of Dillsboro

Konnie Saliba

\* To imitate train wheels, use fingernails on the drum head.
Move hand in a circular motion with the quarter note pulse.

## Performance Suggestions

® Play the bass xylophone, bass metallophone bar or a combination of both ostinatos at all times.
® Other instrumental ostinatos can be played in different groupings; experiment with the following arrangements: only recorders, only alto xylophone, alto xylophone and soprano glockenspiel/alto glockenspiel together, alto xylophone and lower recorder parts together, etc., or have students suggest their own ideas.
® A simple choreographed movement can be created and performed by the non-pitched percussion ensemble.
® A train whistle can be used as an introduction and coda, and intermittently throughout the piece for atmosphere.

## Form

® Begin with a single non-pitched instrument ostinato, such as hand drums, and layer in each part until all of the percussion ostinatos are being played. These ostinatos should continue throughout the piece.
® Play the piece as written.
® To extend the performance, layer ostinato patterns in different ways:
® Sometimes, feature the recorders, or just the lower recorder parts. Another time, feature alto xylophone. Another time, feature glockenspiels. Save using all patterns occurring simultaneously until it seems close to an ending!
® While keeping the non-pitched percussion parts constant, feature different instruments, such as alto xylophone, lower recorders, or glockenspiel as a solo part.
® Continue the percussion ostinatos after the second ending, gradually eliminating instruments one at a time until only one remains.
® Have the last percussionist slow down (ritardando) in the last measure in order to end the piece.

# Instrument Guide

**UNPITCHED PERCUSSION**

 Bell tree

 Bongos

 Cabasa

 Claves

 Conga

 Cowbell

 Drum w/ Beater

 Finger Cymbals

 Guiro

 Hand Drum

 Maracas/Shakers

 Suspended Cymbal

 Tambourine

 Temple Blocks

 Triangle

 Vibraslap

 Wood Block

 Percussion

 Cymbal with Brush

 Hand Clap

 Whip

Log Drum

**BARRED INSTRUMENTS**

| | |
|---|---|
| SG | Soprano Glockenspiel |
| AG | Alto Glockenspiel |
| SM | Soprano Metallophone |
| AM | Alto Metallophone |
| BM | Bass Metallophone |
| SX | Soprano Xylophone |
| AX | Alto Xylophone |
| BX | Bass Xylophone |
| CBX | Contra Bass Bars |

## About the Author

Konnie Saliba is an associate professor of music at the University of Memphis, where she directs the Master of Music program with a concentration in Orff-Schulwerk. She has extensive teaching experience at both the elementary and secondary levels, and is a well-known Orff-Schulwerk consultant in the United States, Canada, Germany, Austria, Finland, and the Dominican Republic.

Ms. Saliba is a past president and national honorary member of the American Orff-Schulwerk Association and the author of numerous publications. In 1996, she was the recipient of the American Orff-Schulwerk Distinguished Service Award.

## Notes